THEN AND THERE SERIES
GENERAL EDITOR
MARJORIE REEVES

D1562810

Pizarro and the Incas

NICHOLAS TATE

Illustrated from contemporary sources

LONGMAN

LONGMAN GROUP LIMITED
Longman House
Burnt Mill, Harlow, Essex, CM20 2JE, England

First published 1982
ISBN 0 582 20547 6

Set in 11/12.5pt Baskerville, Monophoto 169
by Pearl Island Filmsetters (H.K.) Ltd.

Printed in Hong Kong
by Wing Tai Cheung Printing Co. Ltd.

Contents

Boundary of the Inca Empire in 1531
Boundaries between countries today
Andes mountains (land over 2,750 metres)

0   500   1000 1500 km

N

COLOMBIA

Quito
ECUADOR

Tumbes

R. Amazon

Chan Chan

Cuzco
Paracas
PERU

BOLIVIA

Tiahuanaco

PACIFIC
OCEAN

CHILE

SOUTH

ATLANTIC

OCEAN

ARGENTINA

Galapagos
Islands

4

To the Reader

In 1531 a Spanish adventurer with an army of less than 200 men set off on a journey in South America that ended with the defeat of a fascinating people. The adventurer was Francisco Pizarro. The people were the Incas of Peru. Pizarro and his men had gone to Peru because they had heard stories about its great wealth. A few years earlier another Spaniard, Hernando Cortes, had conquered the Aztecs in Mexico. Like him, Pizarro and his followers hoped to find palaces full of gold and silver. They were not to be disappointed.

Their march into the Inca Empire is one of the most daring adventures in history. Atahualpa, the Inca Emperor, ruled an area half the size of Europe. His armies greatly outnumbered Pizarro's tiny force. The route which the Spaniards took lay across the Andes mountains, over a pass 4,000 metres above sea-level. There was a good chance that they would be ambushed and killed. It must have seemed an impossible plan, but it worked. Only hours after their arrival at his headquarters Atahualpa was their prisoner. Twelve months later they took Cuzco, the capital, 1,100 kilometres to the south. Within a short time the whole Empire had fallen. This book tells the story of these exciting events and of the people whose way of life was destroyed.

Words printed in *italics* are explained in the Glossary on page 77.

Opposite: *South America, showing the boundary of the Inca Empire in 1531*

1 The Land

Peru today is the third largest country in South America. You can see where it is on the map on page 4. It is more than five times the size of Great Britain. The land that the Incas ruled was even larger, including parts of the neighbouring countries of Ecuador, Bolivia, Chile and Argentina. To understand the story told in this book you must know something about this land.

Imagine therefore that you are flying over Peru in an aeroplane on a clear sunny day. The photographs on pages 7 and 9 will show you some of the things you might see. This is the land that was ruled by the Incas 450 years ago. It was up mountains like these that Francisco Pizarro and his men climbed for their meeting with the Inca Emperor, Atahualpa. In many ways the country still looks today very much as it did then. Most of Peru is still desert, mountain and jungle. Even in those parts where there are a lot of people, the small villages, the patchwork of fields and the hillside terraces like those on page 13 are just as the Spaniards would have seen them in 1532.

Desert, mountain, jungle – it is important to remember these. They are the clue to Peru's history. We can divide the country into three main zones. Look at the diagram on page 8. Along the Pacific coast, for a distance of 4,000 kilometres, from the north of Peru to the middle of Chile, is one of the driest deserts in the world. In some places no rainfall has ever been recorded and no plant life can be seen. The desert mostly consists of sand dunes and low, rocky hills. This first zone, however, is not completely barren. If you fly along the coast you will notice every so often patches of brilliant green that stand out

A valley in the Andes mountains. In 1531 the Inca Emperor ruled this land

by contrast with the brownness around them. These are the river valleys. The mountains that tower above the desert get some rain. Many rivers rise in these mountains and make their way across the desert to the sea. For thousands of years the water from these rivers has been used to *irrigate* the valleys. It is here that most people on the coast live.

There is another reason why this part of Peru is not as difficult to live in as it seems. The cold sea-current that flows along the whole coast is full of the plants that fish eat. Because of this Peru has some of the best fishing grounds in the world. The vast numbers of fish also attract sea-birds, such as cormorants and pelicans, which live on small islands off the coast. The droppings of these birds, called *guano* – from an Indian word 'guanay', which means 'cormorant' – are a very good *fertiliser*, far better than ordinary manure. With plenty of fish, water and fertilisers this coastal strip has always been able to feed a large number of people.

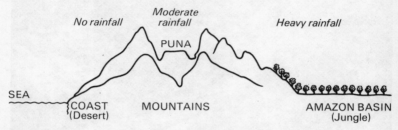

The three main zones of Peru: desert, mountains and jungle

The second zone is the highlands. These are the Andes mountains that run down the whole western side of South America. Much of this region is too high for people to live in. The higher peaks, many of them over 6,000 metres above sea-level, always have snow on them. Most people live in the mountain valleys and in the flat, high *plateaux*, which lie between the mountain ranges. These plateaux, which are called *punas*, are over 3,000 metres above sea-level. They are cold, dry, windswept places, where only tough low grasses and bushes can grow. Each day there is a great change in the temperature, which often rises to 25°C during the day and falls to below freezing point at night. Most crops, except the potato, will not grow well this high up and much of the land is only good for grazing.

The puna is bleak but it is still the part of Peru where most people live. It has a lot of minerals – gold, silver and copper – that were mined long before the Incas. The Indians who live there today somehow manage to make a living for themselves on their small plots of land, growing potatoes and looking

The Andes mountains and the high plateau

after their *llamas*. Large flocks of llamas graze on these desolate plains under the care of their Indian herdsmen, exactly as they did 500 or 1,000 years ago. If Pizarro could return to most parts of the puna today he would think that nothing had changed.

The third zone lies to the east of the Andes. Nearly two-thirds of modern Peru is in this zone, but only eight per cent of the people live there. There are two main parts: the steep, forested mountain slopes and the dense, tropical jungle of the Amazon river basin that lies at their foot. Much of the jungle is still unexplored and inhabited only by tribes of forest Indians. Some of them have never met any people from the outside world.

This, then, is Peru. In some ways, as we have seen, its landscape has changed very little since the time of Pizarro. Of course there are many ways in which it is different. Lima, the

Peruvian Indians today. These farmers still use the same method of drying out their potatoes as their ancestors the Incas did 450 years ago

capital, for example, is a very modern city with a population of over three million people. Its skyscrapers, motorways, supermarkets – and its slums – are like those in other cities all over the world. Pizarro would find all this very strange.

Even on the crowded streets of Lima there is something, however, that reminds the visitor of those events of 450 years ago. Look at the two photographs on page 11. Both these people live in Peru. One is a Spaniard, the other an Indian. Both will probably speak Spanish, though the Indian may speak *Quechua* (pronounced 'ketchooa'), an Indian language, as well. Outside the towns many Peruvian Indians speak only Quechua. If you visited the country today you would soon notice that most of the people are Indians, but many of the important jobs are done by a small number of people of Spanish descent who are often much wealthier than the Indians. There are also, of course, many people of mixed Spanish and Indian blood.

10

An Indian Peruvian   *A Spanish Peruvian*

The reason for this mixture of races lies far back in Peru's history. The Indians, such as the woman above, are, as you will have guessed, the *descendants* of the Incas and of the other native peoples that they ruled over. They speak a language which has probably not changed much since the sixteenth century. The white people are the descendants of the Spanish conquerors and of other people who came from Europe later on.

2 Peru before the Incas

A few years before the coming of the Spaniards the Incas were just a small Indian tribe with no power outside the mountain valley in which they lived. They liked to believe that they were the first civilised people to live in Peru, the first to build cities and roads and to irrigate their fields. This, however, was not true. There had been Indians in this part of South America for many thousands of years before the Incas. For much of this time many of them had been doing the things that the Incas were so proud of. The Indians of Peru, like all the other

Peruvian Indians have used llamas for thousands of years. Llamas are still important to many of them today

The Indians built these terraces so that they could farm the steep mountain slopes of Peru

Indians of North and South America, originally came from Asia. The continents of America and Asia were at one time joined in the far north by a wide plain and men probably crossed over into America when hunting wild animals. They moved slowly southwards until finally they reached Peru.

Gradually these people learnt to grow crops such as beans, *maize* and potatoes. They discovered how to make irrigation ditches so that they could use the water from the rivers flowing through the coastal desert. Later on, in parts of the highlands, they began to build terraces like those above. They could now farm even the steepest mountain slopes. They also *domesticated* animals, especially the guinea-pig and the llama. You may be surprised to know that a lot of their meat came from guinea-pigs. They breed very rapidly and are easy to keep. Indians living in the highlands today still have them in their houses. They feed them on scraps from the tables. They kept llamas for wool as well as for meat, and as pack animals for carrying goods.

13

These Indian farmers also learnt to make pots. They used some of them for cooking and storing. Others were placed in graves next to the body or used in religious ceremonies. Many of these pots are very beautiful. The Indians painted them with complicated patterns or scenes from everyday life and from the lives of their gods. Some have been moulded into different shapes: a man's head, an animal, a bird or a house. Perhaps the most interesting pots are those made by the Mochica people, who lived on the north coast of Peru more than a thousand years before the Incas. You can see a photograph of one of them below. By looking at pots like these we can learn a lot about the people who made them. We can see the animals that were important to them: llamas, guinea-pigs, deer, jaguars and pumas. We can see the birds that they

Left: *A Mochica pot shaped like a man's head*

Below: *A battle scene from a Mochica pot*

14

knew, like the cormorant, the owl and the humming-bird. Here are their gods, shown as animals or birds. Some pots are so life-like that they might have been portraits of actual people. Others show men hunting deer, putting out to sea in canoes, fighting with clubs and spears, playing flutes or walking in processions.

The early farmers in Peru also discovered how to make cloth from cotton and wool. Cotton grows well in many parts of the country and they could get wool from the llama, from the *alpaca*, another tamed animal very like the llama, and from its wild relative, the *vicuña*. They were very skilful makers of cloth. Some of their work is better than anything that machines could make today. Many pieces of cloth have been preserved in the dry sands of the coastal desert. Some are probably as soft and as brightly coloured as when they were made. In 1927 some *archaeologists* discovered a burial place at Paracas on the south coast (see map on page 4). People were probably burying their relatives there around the time of Christ. The archaeologists found 429 *mummies* of elderly men, possibly chieftains and priests, wrapped in clothes of many kinds. Next to them were the weapons, pots and food that the people thought the dead would need in the next world. The magnificent cloaks on these mummies seem to have been made specially for burying people. They are woven in bright colours and decorated with beautiful patterns and with pictures of animals and gods.

These Indians began quite early on to make tools and ornaments out of gold, silver, copper and *bronze*. They also learnt how to build homes for themselves and temples and *pyramids* for their gods. The earliest of these were probably put up between 2000 and 1500 B.C. They were the first large buildings to be built in the whole of North and South America. Later ones, such as the Temples of the Sun and Moon, built by the Mochica people, are even larger. The Temple of the Sun, which you can see on page 16, was perhaps built around A.D. 400 and probably had as many as fifty million mud bricks in it.

The Temple of the Sun. This is how it looks today

Some of these temples and pyramids were parts of large cities. One of the grandest was Tiahuanaco in northern Bolivia. It was built high up on the bleak and treeless puna, nearly 4,000 metres above sea-level with jagged snow-covered peaks on three sides. Huge blocks of stone were used, cut and fitted together with great skill. A Spaniard who visited the ruined city not long after the conquest, wondered 'how human hands could have brought [these stones] to where they now stand'.

By the time the Indians started building temples and cities, much of Peru was already divided up into kingdoms. The kingdoms, however, quarrelled with each other, over land or over the control of water supplies. About 150 years before the Spanish conquest in 1532 two of the Indian peoples tried to conquer large parts of the country. These were the Chimús, who lived on the north coast, and the Incas who came from the southern highlands. A struggle developed between them, in which the Incas eventually triumphed. You can read more about this in the next chapter.

3 The Long March of Topa Inca Yupanqui

The valley of Cuzco lies high up in the Andes, over 3,300 metres above sea-level. It is a large and very beautiful valley, surrounded by mountains. This valley was the first home of the Incas. We do not know when or how they came here. They had certainly been around for at least a few hundred years when the Spaniards arrived in 1532. At first they were just a small and not very important tribe. The lands they ruled were not very large. There were even other tribes living in the same valley. About a hundred years before the coming of the Spaniards, Inca kings and nobles began to make war against their neighbours and to take over their lands. They were not often defeated. Over the years the Inca armies moved further and further away from Cuzco. One by one they forced or persuaded all the other tribes to join their Empire. By 1490 they were ruling the biggest Indian Empire that America had ever seen. The map on page 4 shows you how large it was. Imagine what it was like to be someone living through these events. As a child you had belonged to an unimportant tribe. As an old man or woman you were a citizen of an Empire which you thought covered the whole world.

The Emperor who conquered many of these lands was called Topa Inca Yupanqui. He ruled in Peru from 1471 until he died in 1493. We know more about him than we do about earlier Inca rulers. Some of his soldiers and helpers were still alive when the Spaniards came to Peru and so could tell them what had happened.

The story of Topa Inca's adventures begins in 1463, eight years before he became Emperor. His father, the Emperor

Pachacuti Inca, had done a lot of fighting as a young man, but he was now old and no longer wanted to command the army himself. So he decided to give the command to Topa Inca, his trusted son. Topa Inca's first task was to conquer the northern highlands of Peru. He got together an army from all the lands already ruled by the Incas. Each village sent some men. One by one the groups of soldiers arrived outside Cuzco and put up their tents. Inside the city the Inca priests *sacrificed* llamas to their gods, praying that they would give them a great victory. When everything was ready the long march began, going north through the Andes, across range after range of mountains, deeper and deeper into unknown lands. The army must have looked very impressive as it wound its way through the valleys and over the mountain passes. Try to imagine 250,000 men – all the people living in a middle-sized British city – together with many thousands of llamas, climbing a steep mountain pass in single file. Think how much food this army might have eaten in one day. This should give you some idea of the problems Topa Inca had to face.

The picture opposite shows you what one of the soldiers in this army would have looked like. He is wearing a thick quilted cotton tunic. The padding gave him good protection against spears and stones. (Many Spaniards later preferred them to metal breastplates.) On his head is a helmet, made either of quilted cotton or of wood. Notice also the woollen fringes worn below the knee and around the ankle. These were part of the soldier's uniform, but do not seem to have had any special purpose. On his chest he wears a metal disc. This was a medal awarded for bravery in battle. Some were made of gold, some of silver, and some of bronze. Only soldiers who had shown great bravery were given gold discs to wear. In his left hand he is holding a wooden shield. Some soldiers also wore round shields across their backs, to protect them from an attack from behind.

Look now at the weapons that the Inca soldiers are holding. You should be able to see three main types: the *halberd* (in the front of the picture), the spear and the star-headed mace. Inca

The Incas make war against other tribes. This is a drawing by an Indian artist, Guamán Poma, who lived in Peru after the Spanish conquest

soldiers were especially fond of the mace. It had a round stone or metal head with six points, like a star, and was attached to a wooden handle. It must have done great damage in battle. The Incas also used two long-range weapons: the sling and the *bolas*. Inca slingsmen were so skilful that they could kill a man from a great distance with a single small stone. The bolas is a piece of cord held in the hand and divided into two, three, four or five strings. To each of these strings a stone or metal ball is attached. The whole thing is thrown at the enemy, lashing his arms and legs together and at the same time causing injuries.

As soon as this huge army entered the lands of another tribe, Topa Inca sent messengers to the tribe's leaders, asking them to join the Empire. He let them see how large his army was, to show them how foolish it would be to resist. He promised that no harm would come to them as long as they surrendered. Many tribes agreed. They knew they were too weak to fight the Incas. There were some however who refused to give way. Often they joined together with other tribes to give themselves a better chance of success. The Incas had to fight many battles during this campaign. As you would expect with such a large army they won nearly all of them.

Most battles began with both sides using their slings and bolas. At this stage the two armies were some distance apart. Once these weapons had done some damage, the two sides rushed at each other with loud cries. It was every man for himself, each soldier trying to kill as many of the enemy as he could with his spear and mace. The noise of these battles must have been tremendous. 'They give their mouths no rest when they are fighting', wrote one Spaniard. The Incas shouted at the enemy, sang insulting songs, and made as much noise as they could on their musical instruments. Some of them had single-note trumpets, made either of clay or of sea-shells. Others had flutes made out of bone. They also used drums which were sometimes made from the skins of enemies that they had killed in earlier battles. With all this noise and confusion the soldiers must have had little idea of how the battle was going.

Not all battles were fought in the open. Many of the tribes had built forts on hilltops. They had chosen the sites because of their steep slopes and had *fortified* them with walls and terraces. When the Incas attacked, their enemies retreated

The Emperor Topa Inca Yupanqui

into these forts and rolled large boulders down the hill at anyone who tried to come near. The Incas bombarded them with stones from their slings. Sometimes they heated the stones, dipped them into burning *bitumen* and then aimed them at the thatched roofs of the houses inside the fort. If they thought there was a good chance of success they would make a direct attack on a fort, after it had been weakened in this way. If not, they would simply wait and try to starve the defenders into surrendering.

It was by methods such as these – threats and promises, battles, sieges – that Topa Inca took over one tribe after another. Within a few years he had conquered the whole of the northern highlands, as far north as Quito, the capital of modern Ecuador.

21

An Indian balsa raft. This is a drawing by a Spanish artist

His next step was to take over the northern coast. Most of the Inca soldiers, and probably Topa Inca himself, had never seen the sea before. Imagine their feelings as they saw the great expanse of water, the waves, and the strange sea-birds for the first time. Topa Inca marched southwards along the coast of Ecuador. Eventually he came to the town of Tumbes, where he met some merchants who had arrived by sea from the north. They had travelled on large rafts made of *balsa* logs and fitted with sails. You can see a picture of one of these on this page. They spoke of the land they came from, a land of 'many people and much gold'. Topa Inca was keen to see it for himself. He told his men to build a fleet of balsa rafts. When it was ready he set off northwards into the unknown. This was a very adventurous thing to do. His soldiers were not used to this kind of sailing and did not even have a simple instrument like the compass, which the Spaniards were using at this time. We do not know exactly where Topa Inca went. It was probably just further up the coast of South America, into what is now Colombia. One Spanish writer, however, talks about the 'islands' that he visited. Some historians think that these must have been the Galapagos Islands, 950 kilometres to the west. If this is where he went, it was certainly a very brave and clever thing to have done. There are strong currents in this part of the Pacific Ocean and sailing is very difficult even for experienced sailors using modern instruments.

Topa Inca was away for nearly a year on this voyage. As soon as he returned he made plans to conquer the rest of the north coast. Here were his strongest enemies, the Chimús, who ruled most of this part of Peru. They had built many fortresses and walls to protect themselves from an Inca attack. They were also determined to fight until the very end. The Incas had two big advantages. They were attacking from the north, where the Chimús were not expecting an invasion and where the Chimú defences were weakest. They also controlled the rivers that flow from the mountains down to the coast. This meant that they could stop the Chimús from getting the water they needed to irrigate their fields. The Chimús fought bravely, but in vain. Their capital, Chan Chan, the biggest city ever built in ancient Peru, was occupied by the Incas. Many of their beautiful gold ornaments were seized and sent off to the Emperor in Cuzco. Topa Inca was so impressed by these and by the cloth that the Chimús made that he sent many of their craftsmen to Cuzco as well, to teach their skills to his own people.

Topa Inca now returned to Cuzco. A Spanish writer describes how he entered the city, 'with the greatest, the richest, and the most solemn *triumph* with which any Inca had ever reached the *House of the Sun*, bringing with him people of many different races, strange animals, *innumerable* quantities of riches'. First came the soldiers, marching to the sound of drums and trumpets; then the prisoners, their hands tied behind their backs; then the bearers with all the gold and silver looted during the war; more soldiers with the heads of enemy chieftains on the points of their lances; Inca noblemen; young girls singing and dancing; and last of all Topa Inca, seated in a *litter*, with other members of his family. When they had all reached the great square in the centre of Cuzco, the prisoners were made to lie on the ground. Topa

23

Inca got down from his litter and walked across their bodies to show that he was their conqueror. After this there were dances, banquets, mock battles and sacrifices to the gods. These probably continued for many days.

Topa Inca did not stay in Cuzco for very long. He soon set off on another successful expedition, this time against the peoples who lived on the south coast of Peru. It was soon after this second campaign that his father, the old Emperor, decided to resign and hand over the Empire to his son. This was in 1471. Topa Inca ruled for another twenty-two years until his death in 1493. There were many other wars during his reign. Most were successful. He forced many other tribes to join the Inca Empire. We do not know exactly how many kilometres Topa Inca marched during his life. It must have been at least 15,000. Look again at the map on page 4. This will give you an idea of the size of the Empire at the end of his reign. It stretched for 4,000 kilometres from Ecuador in the north to Chile in the south. For most Incas this Empire was the whole world. They knew nothing about other continents and very little about other parts of South America. To them Topa Inca was the conqueror of the world.

Topa Inca and his father had to rule their lands as well as fight. This was not easy. The Empire, as we have seen, included many lands and peoples. Only very clever and determined rulers could have held it together. How did the Incas do it?

One way was to build roads. This made sure that soldiers could be moved quickly to any trouble-spot. The Empire was soon covered with a network of roads like the one opposite. The two most important ones ran the whole length of the Empire, from Ecuador to Chile, one through the highlands, the other along the coast. The highland roads were marvels of engineering. On steep slopes the builders cut steps out of the rock. When they came to a wide river they built suspension bridges out of twigs twisted together. No country was too difficult for them. They also built storehouses every few kilometres, for the use of soldiers and travelling officials.

Along the main roads they had a very good postal service. Every quarter of a league (about 1 kilometre) they built a pair of huts, one on each side of the road. Each hut sheltered two runners. The runners were part of a relay system. When they saw another runner coming towards their hut, one of them got ready to join him and then ran alongside him until he received the message. This might be either spoken or recorded on a *quipu* (you will read about these in Chapter 4). He then ran as fast as he could to the next hut where the next runner was also waiting. In this way the runners carried messages at an average speed of 240 kilometres a day. One Spanish writer tells us that the relay system was also used as a way of bringing the Emperor fresh fish from the coast.

Look again at the picture below and try to imagine what this stretch of road would have been like in the days of the Incas. From time to time a runner perhaps would pass. He might be carrying an important message from Cuzco, on its way to some town in another part of the Empire. Then there were bands of soldiers, off to put down a rebellion or to fight another war on the borders of the Empire. Sometimes an important official passed by in his litter. Many travellers were ordinary people. They might be taking things such as

The Incas built this road in Peru over 450 years ago

wood, cloth, pottery or vegetables to the local market. The Incas had not invented the wheel and so people either had to carry everything themselves or load it into saddle-bags on the backs of llamas. Long trains of llamas moved slowly along these roads. The llama that led the procession always had bells on its saddle, its neck and its ears. In the silence of the mountains the tinkling of these bells was often the only sound you would hear.

The Incas knew that the roads were not enough by themselves to keep their Empire together. They also had to persuade the other tribes that Inca rule was not such a bad thing after all. Many of these tribes at first disliked being ruled by 'foreigners'. They were perhaps not very happy when they were told to worship the Inca gods, as well as their own. There were times when the Incas seemed cruel. On the whole, however, the Incas made sure that the people they ruled did not have too much to complain about. They even gave food and clothing to tribes they had conquered. If they did not trust a tribe the Incas moved them to another part of the Empire, where they would be less troublesome. Many were moved to Cuzco. Here they could be closely watched. In their place the Emperor sent groups of Incas to form *colonies* of loyal subjects. The Incas also encouraged everyone in the Empire to speak Quechua, their own language. By the time that the Spaniards arrived in Peru many of the other Indian languages were disappearing.

When Topa Inca died in 1493 his son, Huayna Capac, became Emperor. The fighting continued. The only people the Incas could not defeat were the warlike Indians who lived to the east of the Andes. The Inca soldiers were used to fighting in the mountains and found it very difficult to get to grips with an enemy in the tropical jungle.

From these tribes living to the east of the Andes the Incas first heard stories of the white men who had recently come to other parts of South America. The first European to reach the Inca Empire in fact came from the east. He was a soldier called Alejo Garcia, a survivor of an unsuccessful Spanish

The Inca Emperor Huayna Capac standing in his war litter during a battle. Notice the sling in his right hand

expedition to the east coast of South America. He had heard from the Indians about a Great King who lived far away to the west. He set out to try and find him. With only three or four companions and a large band of more or less friendly Indians, he travelled for nearly 3,000 kilometres through forests, across swamps and over mountains. At last he reached the plateau of Bolivia. Here he fought with his Indian allies against the Incas. On his way back to the coast the Indians turned against him and killed both him and his companions. No news therefore reached Spain of what he had found. But the Incas had seen these strangers for the first time. Imagine the excitement there must have been when the news arrived in Cuzco. Not long afterwards news also reached Huayna Capac that white men had come across the sea in a strange ship and landed at Tumbes in the north of the Empire. The commander of these men was Francisco Pizarro.

4 Son of the Sun

'One and only Inca', 'Son of the Sun', 'Lover of the poor', 'Most powerful Lord'. These are some of the names that the Indians gave to their Emperor. When they said 'Son of the Sun', they really meant it. They believed that the Sun was a god and that their Emperor was a child of this god. They certainly treated him like one. People who went to see him had to take off their sandals and put a kind of weight on their backs. They bowed down before him, keeping their eyes fixed on the ground so as not to look into his face. They then stretched out their arms, just as they did when they prayed to their gods, made a strange clicking sound with their lips and kissed their fingertips. After this they told him their message. Often the Emperor sat behind a screen to make it quite certain that they would not see him. Visitors even sometimes had to stand with their backs to him. You can imagine how nervous some people must have been when they went before the Emperor. One nobleman trembled so much he could not even stand up. We know this because one of the first Spaniards to go to Peru met him and wrote about it in the story of his adventures.

Some Indians of course were able to look at the Emperor. These were his important officials, his generals and members of his own family. If you had been one of these, or an ordinary Indian who managed to catch a glimpse of him, what would you have seen? The picture opposite will give you some idea. As you can see, the Emperor is sitting on a stool on top of a high platform. In his hand he holds a mace. He is wearing a tunic and cape made from very fine vicuña wool. In his ears are huge golden ear-plugs. Around the top of his head he

The Inca Emperor on his throne, surrounded by noblemen

wears a brightly coloured headdress. From this hangs a fringe
of red tassels fixed to little golden tubes. The headdress also
supports a stick with a kind of pompon attached to it and,
right at the top, three black and white feathers from the wings
of a rare bird. Anyone seeing this headdress could tell at a   29

glance that they were looking at the Emperor. It had the same kind of purpose as the crowns that kings wore in Europe. Whenever the Emperor walked anywhere two attendants, each carrying a mace, went with him. Another attendant held the royal flag. Crowds of officials and servants would also follow him. People seeing him would cry aloud 'Most great and mighty Lord, Son of the Sun, you alone are our Lord'. It must have been a splendid sight.

For much of the time the Emperor lived in his palace in Cuzco. Each Emperor had a new palace built specially for him. All the other relatives of the old Emperor stayed on in the old palace. By the time the Spaniards arrived in Peru there had been twelve Inca Emperors. This is why there were so many palaces in Cuzco. Each one belonged to the descendants of one of the Emperors. They built them of stone or of clay and straw bricks called *adobes*. Sometimes they covered the walls with plates of gold. If we can believe one writer, an Inca prince called Garcilaso who later went to live in Spain, they even used gold and silver as *mortar* to pour into the cracks between the stones. Around the palaces were beautiful gardens and orchards, full of plants, trees and animals made from silver and gold. Inside the palace it was the same. There were

An Inca craftsman made this silver model of an alpaca

gold statues around the walls; even the bath tubs were made of gold. No wonder the Spaniards couldn't believe their eyes.

Some of the palaces were very large. Garcilaso remembered seeing one which had a hall 'so large that sixty mounted men could easily *joust* in it'. They had to be big to hold all the people who lived or worked there. Each Emperor had dozens of wives, and many children as well. Besides these there were all his officials and servants to cook the food, sweep the floors, carry the water and look after the garden. Most servants only stayed in the royal palace for a few weeks at a time. They came from the villages near Cuzco and took it in turns to work for the Emperor. One village provided all the gardeners, another all the woodcutters, and so on.

The Emperor's wives prepared all his food. They served it to him on gold and silver plates which they put on a mat at his feet. The Emperor pointed to the dish that he wanted to eat. One of his wives then held it in front of him while he took out the food with his fingers. They saved the leftovers and later burnt them all. They also burnt all his used clothes. You may find this surprising, but remember this is a god, not a man, we are talking about. At least that is what the Incas thought their Emperor was.

The Emperor spent many hours each day with his officials. There were a lot of things to talk about. How many soldiers did they need for the war in the north? Should they build a new road down to the coast? How much food would they have to send to one of the provinces where there was a famine? Every day messengers and officials arrived from all parts of the Empire. Some just brought gifts. Others came to ask the Emperor's advice or had something important to tell him. Most of these officials were noblemen. These were a very special group of people who were much better off than ordinary Indians. They owned a lot of land. They took all the important jobs. They even thought they would go to heaven when they died, however wicked they had been during their lives. (Ordinary people of course would only go to heaven if they had been good.)

There were two ways to become a nobleman in Peru. You were either born one, or the Emperor made you one. The most important noblemen were the descendants of the Emperors. These were the *orejones* (pronounced 'orrayhonays') or 'big ears', as the Spaniards called them. They got this name because they were the only people, apart from the Emperor, who were allowed to wear plugs in their ears. They were also the only ones who could wear a head-band like the Emperor's. Orejones became generals, rulers of provinces and advisers to the Emperor. Less important than these were the 'chiefs'. They were the rulers of little districts all over the Empire. Some ruled 10,000 families, some 1,000 and some 100. Many of them were noblemen from other Indian tribes that the Incas had conquered. The Incas had let them keep their lands and made them into officials. Their job was to collect all the food from the Emperor's lands, to raise an army if one were needed, and to punish criminals. Most were able to pass their job on to one of their sons when they died.

Whatever kind of nobleman you were, you had to go to school. This was to train you for the important job you would do when you grew up. Only the children of noblemen went to school in Peru, and then only the boys. A few girls went to places a bit like *convents*. You will read about these in Chapter 5. Women however never became officials. The only schools were in Cuzco. This was quite deliberate. The Incas knew that chiefs were not going to cause trouble while their sons were hostages in the capital. School lasted for four years, probably from the age of ten to the age of fourteen. In the first year the children learnt Quechua, the language of the Incas, if they did not know it already. In the second year they learnt about the gods. In the third year they were taught how to use the knotted strings or quipu that you see on page 33. In the fourth year they studied Inca history.

It was especially important that boys who were going to be officials should know how to use a quipu. The Incas had not learnt to write and the quipu was about the only way they had of recording numbers. You can see from the picture that

it was a long cord with a lot of smaller woollen threads tied
to it. Officials recorded a number by tying knots in one of the
threads. Every year Inca officials counted the number of
people in their districts. They added up the totals, recorded
them on the quipus and sent them to the Emperor in Cuzco.
This helped him decide how much tax each part of his Empire
should pay and how many soldiers it should send to his army.

When they had finished their training all the boys took part
in an important ceremony to show that they had come of age.
This happened every December. There was a lot of feasting
and dancing. They made sacrifices to the gods, ran races and
wrestled with each other. Relatives gave each boy a shield,
a mace and a sling. They were now warriors and men. If
they were from one of the royal families, they also had their
ears pierced and wore gold ear-plugs for the first time. After
this, the sons of chiefs went back to their homes all over the
Empire. They now helped their fathers in their jobs. In time
they became chiefs themselves.

Every so often the Emperor went on a tour of his empire.
His chief wife, the *Coya*, usually went with him. They travelled 33

Topa Inca Yupanqui riding in a litter with his chief wife, the Coya

together, sitting opposite each other in a litter as in the picture above. For most of the journey the curtains at the sides of the litter were closed, so people along the road could not catch a glimpse of the Emperor. The curtains had little holes in them, so the Emperor and the Coya could see without being seen. The Indians who carried the Emperor's litter always came from the same two provinces. There were sometimes as many as twenty-five of them carrying the litter at the same time. This made sure that if one of them stumbled, the Emperor would hardly notice. There were severe punishments however for anyone who did stumble. Other Indians went ahead to sweep the road. They even removed all the blades of grass along the Emperor's path.

When an Emperor died the Incas believed he had gone back to live with his father, the Sun. His wives cut their hair short, blackened their faces and walked through the streets weeping and crying aloud. Sometimes wives and servants were killed so they could carry on looking after the Emperor in the next world. Like the ancient Egyptians the Incas preserved the Emperor's body. It stayed in its palace in Cuzco and servants continued to look after it as if it were alive. From time to time they put it on a litter and carried it through the streets. Sometimes they looked after the body of the Coya in the same way.

Each Emperor had many sons and it was not always easy to decide which of them was to take over when he died. In order to avoid squabbling many Emperors told everyone which son they had chosen. They even crowned him with the headdress during their own lifetime. One Emperor who did not do this was Huayna Capac. He died so suddenly that there was no time for him to announce who was going to be the new Emperor. This helped the Spaniards, as you will find out.

5 Cuzco the Holy City

'The great city of Cuzco' – this is what one Indian writer later called the capital of the Incas. His name was Guamán Poma and you have already looked at some of his drawings of Inca life. His picture of Cuzco is on page 39.

The Incas thought that Cuzco was the centre of the world. In the middle of the city was a big square called Huacapata. This is where the triumph that you read about in Chapter 3 took place. The Incas thought of their Empire as a kind of circle. This square was its centre. Like spokes from the hub of a wheel four roads led out of the square on their way to the furthest parts of the Empire. As you can see from the diagram, these four roads divided the Empire into four quarters, each with its own name

Plan of Cuzco, the capital city of the Incas

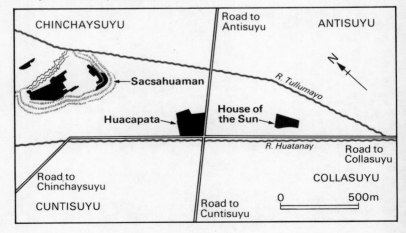

The ruins of the Inca fortress of Sacsahuaman in Cuzco today

(e.g. Antisuyu). They also divided the city into four quarters. Each of these had the same name as the part of the Empire it belonged to. When visitors came to Cuzco from the provinces the Incas only allowed them to stay in their own quarter. They also forbade them to live in the centre of the city. Only the Emperor and the orejones, and their servants, could live there.

You can see from the diagram that the centre of Cuzco was built on a triangle of land between two small rivers. Inside this triangle the Incas had deliberately laid out their city in the shape of a *puma*. Some of them believed that this animal was a god. The huge stone fortress of Sacsahuaman was the puma's head. Its tail was a narrow strip of garden where the two rivers met. The great square was the space between the puma's front and back legs. Other squares, palaces, houses and temples made up the rest of its body. In between these buildings were many narrow paved streets. Each had a stone channel down the middle, for carrying water to the houses. Every day many people and animals would pass along these dark streets between the thick stone walls of the palaces. You might have seen a proud Inca nobleman in his brightly 37 coloured tunic and cloak, followed by two or three of his servants; or a visiting chieftain from the provinces, bringing gifts to the Emperor. There would be farmers from nearby villages, bent double under the weight of fruit or vegetables that they were taking to the storehouses of the Emperor. Women would pass by, their long dresses almost touching the ground. Some might be carrying babies in cradles tied by a shawl to their backs. Amongst all these people you might have seen a long line of snow-white llamas, brought into the city to be sacrificed to the Inca gods.

We do not know exactly how many people lived in Cuzco. As the Incas had not learnt to write there are no Indian records that we can look at. The city was also burnt to the ground in 1535 during the war between the Spaniards and the Incas. Very few Spaniards therefore visited it before it was destroyed. None of them was able to make an exact count of the number of people who lived there. One of the few Spaniards who did visit the city before it was burnt said that there were about four thousand buildings in the triangle between the two rivers. It must therefore have been quite a big city, as big as many in Europe at that time. Another Spaniard wrote that it was 'so large and beautiful that it would be worthy to appear even in Spain'.

There was much more to Cuzco than the part between the two rivers where the orejones lived. Surrounding the city were fields and gardens and some of the terraces that you read about in Chapter 2. Beyond these were many more houses, palaces, and whole villages, built on the slopes of the valley. Here were the country houses of the orejones and the houses of visiting chieftains, forbidden to live in the city itself. Here were the farmers who grew maize, fruit and vegetables for the great lords of the city. Many of these farmers had come from faraway parts of the Empire. The Incas had brought them here to keep an eye on them. You could tell which province they came from by their different clothes. Here also were the great storehouses in which the Emperor kept the food and the cloth that the people sent him from all the provinces of the

Guamán Poma's drawing of Cuzco, showing its temples, palaces and squares

Empire. There were the temples as well and other holy places of the Inca gods. One Spaniard said that there must have been as many as 100,000 buildings in this valley. This might be a bit exaggerated, but every year archaeologists are digging up more of them.

For many Indian visitors to Cuzco the most important buildings were the temples of the gods. Cuzco was a holy city.

There were 350 temples or holy places in or around Cuzco, almost one for every day in the year. The biggest and most important was the Temple of the Sun. This was in fact a number of stone temples, built round a courtyard. The temple of the sun god was the main one. The Incas worshipped many gods. One of them was called *Viracocha*. They thought of him as a man with a beard. They believed that he had made the whole world and taught man how to grow crops and make cloth. He had then disappeared across the sea. One day he would return. Meanwhile the world continued because he wanted it to. Viracocha therefore was the chief of the gods. The Incas made a statue of him as a man. They placed it in the Temple of the Sun and worshipped him there. In their everyday lives, however, the Sun God was much more important. His son, the Emperor, lived among them. They could actually see him in the sky. He gave them light and made their crops grow. They had to please him to make sure that he did not go away. This is why the Incas built Temples of the Sun in all the cities of their Empire. In Cuzco they covered the doors and walls of his temple in gold. This of course was the sun's colour. Some Incas even believed that the gold they found in the ground was the tears of the sun. Inside the temple, fixed to a wall, was a huge gold disc, made to look like the sun. It had the face of a man and many golden rays round the edges. Next to this disc were the preserved bodies of the dead Emperors, each sitting on his throne. These were the sons of the Sun. The Incas had brought them here to live in their father's house. They must have looked like big dolls without arms or legs.

To please the Sun God the Incas sacrificed a llama to him in the great square of Cuzco on every day of the year, at sunrise, at noon, and at sunset. They were afraid that if they did not do this, the sun would stop moving through the sky. The Incas also held a number of big festivals each year in honour of their god. The most important of these was the Feast of the Sun, in June. On the first day of the feast the Inca nobles met before dawn in an open space just to the east of

the city. The orejones were there, dressed in long red robes.
So too were the bodies of the dead Emperors, propped up
inside tents made of feathers. On another side were all the
chieftains from the provinces. It was still dark. Everyone looked
anxiously towards the east, where the sun was about to rise.
When all were ready the Emperor arrived, carried through
the crowd in a golden litter. The procession stopped, the
Emperor got down and walked slowly over to a throne. Here
he sat, looking towards the east. No one spoke. As the first
rays appeared above the top of the hill he stood up and walked
towards his father, the Sun, holding out his arms and singing
quietly a special hymn. Everyone else lay down on the ground,
their hands stretched out towards the rising sun. The Emperor
and his priests then made many sacrifices to the god. They
offered him cups of *chicha*, a drink made from maize, pouring
the liquid on to the ground. They sacrificed many llamas as
well. They kept the blood and hearts for the sun and then
burnt what was left. They very carefully saved the ashes from   41

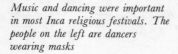

Music and dancing were important in most Inca religious festivals. The people on the left are dancers wearing masks

The Feast of the Sun in Cuzco. The Incas offer the maize drink, chicha, to the Sun God

these fires. Later in the year they would throw them into the water at the place where the two rivers met. Sometimes they even sacrificed children and young people in this way. After the sacrifices there was dancing, singing and feasting. This went on for many days.

The Incas worshipped other gods besides Viracocha and the Sun. The Moon, Venus, the stars called the Pleiades, and the rainbow, all had temples of their own inside the Temple of the Sun. The Incas thought that the Moon was the wife of the Sun. On the wall of her temple was a great silver disc. In other places there were temples to Mother Earth, to the Thunder God, and to the Sea. They worshipped many other things as well, such as stones with strange shapes, bridges, hills, caves, and the tombs of their *ancestors*. Every day the Incas came across something that was special, something they had to be careful about. They were always making sacrifices. These were usually just a few drops of chicha which they poured over the ground. The Incas were a very religious people. They did very little without thinking about their gods.

42

There were a lot of priests in Inca Peru, but ordinary people were able to make sacrifices to the gods themselves. They needed priests, however, to look after the temples and to make special sacrifices. All over the Empire the Incas set aside a lot of land, called 'the lands of the Sun', for the priests. Ordinary people had to look after the crops on this land. At harvest time they took the maize and the potatoes from these fields to big storehouses. Only priests could use this food.

In some temples there were priestesses as well. Women always looked after the temples of the Moon Goddess. There were some, called 'The Chosen Women', who spent all their lives in special houses or convents, worshipping the sun. They did not marry and almost never left their convent. They wove cloth and made sacrifices. They were also teachers. The daughters of noblemen spent a few years at one of these convents. The Chosen Women taught them about the gods and how to spin, weave and cook.

If you were ill you might go to a *sorcerer*, just as you would go to a doctor today. His job was to cure your disease by magic. You might also visit him if you wanted to harm an enemy. The sorcerer would take a big doll, put inside it things belonging to the person you wanted to hurt, such as hairs and bits of finger-nails, and then prick it with thorns. Sorcerers would also try to make someone else fall in love with you. Some of them guessed what was going to happen in the future. There were many different ways of doing this. They listened for voices in the fire. They looked at the insides of animals they had sacrificed. Some could tell everything by watching how spiders moved across the floor.

6 Village Life

Amaro is an Indian farmer. He is thirty-eight years old. His name is the Quechua word for 'dragon'. He lives in a small village on the slopes of a mountain valley about 300 kilometres from Cuzco. He has only left his village twice. The first time was when he got orders to help build a road down on the coast. The other time was a miserable six months he spent working in a gold mine high up in the Andes. He hopes it will be some time before he has to go and work away from home again. So of course does his wife, Qori, (her name means 'gold'), his daughter, Ronto ('egg'), who is twelve, and his son, Sinci ('strong'), who is eight. Amaro and Qori also have a baby daughter. She will not get a name until Qori stops breast-feeding her. This will probably be when she is two years old.

The picture on the next page shows you what Amaro and Qori and their daughter look like. Qori is wearing a long plain dress, tied by a very wide sash at the waist. Over her shoulders she sometimes wears a cloak which she fastens at the front with a bronze pin. Both the cloak and the dress are made from alpaca wool. On her head is a simple headdress. By looking at the colour and shape of this headdress any Indian could tell which part of the Empire she comes from. The Incas had a rule that everyone in the same district wore the same clothes. They punished anyone who broke it. Amaro's clothes are very similar to Qori's. His tunic and his cloak, however, are shorter. Both sometimes wear sandals. Like their clothes, they make these themselves. They use llama skins for the soles and plaited llama wool for the straps.

44   The family, their two dogs and large numbers of guinea-

Inca farmers plant their maize. The man is using a taklla or foot plough

pigs, live in a small square hut. The villagers built it for Amaro and Qori when they got married. They made the walls out of large stones plastered together with mud. They put on a wooden roof and thatched it with long grass. When the thatch needs repairing it is Sinci and Ronto's job to go out and cut more grass. The hut has only one room, no windows and no smoke hole. You have to bend down to get in through the door. Inside it is very dark. When Qori is cooking it can be very smoky as well. At one end of the hut, on the earth floor, is a pile of woollen blankets and llama skins for the family to sit and sleep on. They all sleep huddled up together, still wearing their day clothes. They store their food and drink in big clay jars and boxes made out of straw and plaster. They have also dug a pit in the floor and plastered it with mud. This is where they keep their grain. Against the wall are the tools that they use out in the fields. Their home is one of six huts built round a small courtyard. Grandparents, sisters, brothers, uncles and aunts live in the others.

There are plenty of jobs to do on the land. When Amaro and Qori got married their chief gave them a pair of llamas

45

and a small part of the village lands on which to grow their crops. He gave them extra bits of land when each of their three children was born. Like everyone else they have just enough land to feed themselves. Later on, when the children leave home, some of this land will be taken away.

All the land in the village belongs to the Emperor. It is only because of his kindness that Amaro and the other farmers can use it for themselves. This, at least, is what their chief has always told them. In return, however, they have to look after the 'lands of the Sun' that you read about in Chapter 5 and the Emperor's own lands. This means a great deal of extra work. But Amaro doesn't grumble. This is work for the gods; it has to be done. He also feels that, in a way, it is for his own good. When the harvest is over, the people take all the Emperor's crops to storehouses in the village or the nearest town. Some of it even goes to Cuzco. The Emperor uses the food for himself and the orejones, for all their servants, and for his army. There is a lot left over, however, and this is saved to give to the poor or to send to provinces where there is a famine. Once, when Amaro was a young man, it did not rain for six months and most people in his village lost all their crops. When the Emperor's officer, in the nearby town of Vilcas, heard about this he quickly sent them all the food they needed and no one starved. The Incas organised this kind of help far better than most countries in Europe at the same time.

As well as looking after the Emperor's land and the lands of the Sun, Amaro, like all Indian men aged between twenty-five and fifty, also has to spend up to five years of his life working in other ways for the Emperor. They call this work the *mita*. It might mean building roads or working down the mines; Amaro has done this already. Some men go to Cuzco as servants in the Emperor's palaces. Others work in the stone quarries, build bridges, palaces and fortresses or look after the Emperor's big herds of llamas and alpacas high up in the puna. Many go to be soldiers in the army.

This year at least Amaro expects to be free to work on his own land. He has already helped with ploughing and sowing the lands of the Emperor and the Sun. After a few days working on the chief's lands, and helping those families where the husband has died or is away on the mita, he at last gets permission to start work on his own land. He has three fields just below the village. There is not much of it, but the soil is good.

The farming year begins in September. This is when Amaro and Qori plant their maize. After fertilising the land with llama dung or human manure, they begin to plough. Amaro does this with the *taklla* or foot plough that you saw in the picture on page 45. The taklla is still used in Peru today, as you can see from the photograph below. Qori follows him across the field, breaking up large clods of earth with a *hoe*. Amaro then uses his taklla to make holes for the seed. Qori throws in the seeds and Ronto scrapes the earth over them with a wooden board shaped like a boat. Maize is their main crop; it grows well on the warm lower slopes of the valley. They grow other crops as well: beans, *chili peppers*, which they

A Peruvian boy using a taklla or foot plough in modern Peru

47

put in all their stews and soups, *quinua*, which is a kind of rice, and of course, potatoes which they plant higher up the valley and on the puna, where maize will not grow.

September, October and November are usually very dry months in this part of Peru. Maize needs water all the time, so Amaro and the other villagers have to irrigate their land. Many years ago a large number of mita workers dug irrigation channels all over the fields. These all link up with a big stream that flows down the side of the valley. When the villagers need water all they have to do is to open the *sluice-gates* and turn the water into the irrigation channels. Sometimes the

Irrigating the fields during the dry season

rains are late and there is not enough water in the stream. When this happens all the villagers go out into the fields, banging gongs to frighten away the drought, and calling on the Thunder God to send them rain.

The rains usually start in December and continue on and off until March. During these hot, wet months the crops grow quickly. Amaro and his family are busy in the fields, weeding and driving away birds and animals, such as foxes and skunks,

48

that might harm the crops. Sinci and Ronto are often out in the fields all day, shaking a big stick covered with rattles and tassels, banging drums and firing stones at the birds with their slings. Qori and the other women also take turns to spend the night in a little straw hut that the villagers have built out in the fields. All night long she bangs her drum to scare away

Inca farmers protect their maize from pests

the pests. The villagers do not worry too much about human thieves. There are such strict punishments for stealing that most people are too frightened to try. Any theft from the Emperor's land is especially serious. The punishment for this is always death, by hanging or stoning.

In May the maize is harvested. This is usually a happy time of year, especially if the harvest is good. The villagers go out to the fields, dancing and singing to the sound of flutes, tambourines and bells. They make sacrifices to the gods and when all the grain has been collected and stored away they spend three days and nights in feasting. In June they harvest the potatoes. The Indians do not have any carts so they have to carry the crop back to their houses themselves or on their llamas.

Qori is very busy at this time of year, grinding the maize grain into flour so that it will keep. She also has a clever way of drying out the potatoes for the same reason. Most of the things that the family use they make themselves. They make their own ropes, for example, out of llama wool, their own spoons and needles out of llama bones, their own combs out of thorns and pieces of wood, their cooking-pots and dishes, clothes, sandals, and much more besides. The family eat twice a day, at about eight o'clock in the morning, and one or two hours before sunset. The meal is usually a soup or stew, made from maize, potatoes and beans and flavoured with herbs and chili peppers. Sometimes they eat a little guinea-pig or llama meat. Chicha is their main drink. By evening they are usually very tired. They sit on the floor of the hut with their food, often not speaking to each other for minutes on end.

One evening when they are in the middle of a meal they hear the noise of voices outside in the courtyard. Amaro gets up and puts his head out of the doorway. There, surrounded by a group of people all talking excitedly, is a man he has hoped not to see again for some time. It is one of the Emperor's officers from Vilcas. He has come with bad news. A war has broken out between the Emperor and his brother. More soldiers are needed. Amaro is one of those chosen to go and fight.

7 The Spaniards Arrive

Many years earlier, around the time when Amaro was born, three ships set sail from Spain on an important journey. The man in charge of these ships was an Italian called Christopher Columbus. You can read about how he reached America in another Then and There book called 'The Voyages of Christopher Columbus'.

Amaro, in his village in Peru, knew nothing about Columbus. Not even the Inca Emperor and his officials had any idea of what was happening further north in the Caribbean Sea. One person who did – a long way from Peru – was a Spaniard named Francisco Pizarro. He was quite a lot older than Amaro, born probably around 1475. As a young man, living on his father's farm in a poor part of Spain, he heard exciting reports of the lands that Columbus had reached across the sea. He knew that if he stayed at home he would probably be poor all his life. So he decided to seek his fortune in America. He arrived on the island of Hispañiola in the Caribbean in 1502 (see map on page 57). Like other Spaniards he was looking for gold and silver and so he joined one of the exploring expeditions which set out from the island.

This was in 1509, along the coast of what is now Colombia. The explorers built one of the first Spanish settlements on the mainland. It was a complete disaster. Within a few months most of the men were dead, from starvation and disease or from the poisoned arrows of the Indians. Pizarro and the other survivors, led by a man named Balboa, left the settlement and moved along the coast to a place where there was more food and fewer fierce Indians. Hearing from some Indians

51

about another ocean to the south, next to which were lands full of gold, Balboa set off inland. The mainland here was only 80 kilometres wide, but full of swamps, forests and dangerous Indian tribes. At last, after weeks of travelling, he caught his first glimpse of the Pacific Ocean, glinting in the sun beneath him. He waded into the sea, holding in his hands the flag of Spain and claiming for the Spanish King the Pacific Ocean and all the lands around it. Not long afterwards Balboa quarrelled with the Spanish governor at Darién and was beheaded.

Balboa's death did not put a stop to exploration. Others explored the Pacific coast northwards as far as Nicaragua. Pizarro himself took part in a small expedition to the Pearl Islands off the Pacific coast. The Indians on these islands were at first friendly but the Spaniards treated them very badly, burning their huts, killing them or carrying them off to the mainland as slaves. One report tells how some of their chiefs were torn to pieces by the fierce dogs the Spaniards brought with them. These dogs went on most Spanish expeditions. They soon got used to the taste of human flesh.

In 1519 the Spaniards built the small town of Panama on the Pacific coast and Pizarro went to live there. He was the town's first mayor. He had a lot of land and some Indians to look after it for him. He was not, however, a rich man, and was therefore very interested in the stories that kept on reaching Panama of a great kingdom to the south, full of silver and gold. He also heard in 1520 of how the Spanish captain, Hernando Cortes, had conquered the great and rich Empire of the Aztecs in Mexico with only a handful of men. If Cortes had won wealth and fame by marching into Mexico, why should not Pizarro do the same by sailing southwards?

This is in fact what he did, but it took him much longer than it had taken Cortes. Pizarro, however, was not the kind of man to give up easily. One of the main problems was money. For his first expedition, in 1524–5, Pizarro sought the help

Opposite: *Francisco Pizarro, a contemporary painting*

D. FRAN.^{co} PIZARRO.

Pizarro and Almagro set off from Panama on their journey to Peru. They swear an oath in front of their friend, Fernando de Luque, promising to share with him all the riches they gain

of two of his friends in Panama, Diego de Almagro and Fernando de Luque. Almagro was another tough adventurer from the same part of Spain. Luque was a priest and schoolmaster. Luque seems to have provided most of the money. Pizarro and Almagro were to do most of the work. They were all to share in the profits. The expedition however was a failure. Strong winds stopped them from sailing very far down the coast. When they landed all they found were swamps and forests and fierce Indian tribes who soon drove them back to their ships. Many men were killed and Almagro lost an eye in an Indian attack.

On their return they persuaded the Governor of Panama to help them to make a second expedition. This sailed in 1526. At first things did not go very well. Pizarro and Almagro wasted time wandering through the *mangrove* swamps along the Colombian coast. Again, many men died from starvation or in Indian attacks. One of their two ships, however, sailed southwards as far as what is now Ecuador (see map on page 57). Here at sea they came across an Inca raft, like the ones you read about in Chapter 3. This had come from the town of Tumbes. It was carrying fine cloth and objects of gold and silver, for sale to the Indians of Ecuador. The Inca merchants on the raft told the Spaniards of much greater riches further south. When the Spanish ship returned with this news, Pizarro and Almagro were keen to explore further. They had very few men by this time, so Almagro returned to Panama to persuade others to join them. Pizarro meanwhile waited with his men on an island off the coast. Here they had a miserable few months, with heavy rain, swarms of mosquitoes and hardly any food. By this time many of the men were keen to get back to Panama. Some of them had smuggled messages back on

An old model of the kind of ship used by Pizarro

Almagro's ship, asking the Governor to send a ship to rescue them. One of these was from a barber-surgeon who had gone with the expedition (Spanish barbers were often also surgeons in those days). 'I'm very well', he wrote to his brother, 'please ask the Governor... to give me permission to come to Panama, since I have done all I am obliged to, and am married, and they have held me by force for more than a year and a half'. The Governor took pity on him and sent a rescue ship. When it arrived at Gallo Island most of the men, said one Spanish writer, '*embarked* with great joy'. Only twelve agreed to stay with Pizarro to wait for Almagro's return. Almagro, however, had not been able to persuade any other Spaniards to join him. When, after another seven months, he finally rejoined Pizarro, it was only with a ship, a few sailors, and some Indian slaves. With these they sailed southwards and after a lot of difficulties reached the town of Tumbes. At last, after all these years, they were inside the Inca Empire itself. They were amazed at the large buildings and at the gold and the silver. They were even more excited by the stories they heard of a sun god king who lived high up in the dome of the sky. After a long journey to the south they sailed back up the coast to Panama, thinking of only one thing – how they would soon return with a large force to conquer the rich lands they had found.

Nothing was ever easy for Pizarro. He had no money left for another expedition, and few people in Panama believed the stories he told them. The Governor refused to help him. The only hope was to go to Spain, to see the Emperor Charles (who was King of Spain). Somehow he found the money to pay for his journey. He took with him samples of Inca cloth and gold and silver work, a few Indians, and some llamas, as proof of the riches he had discovered. He arrived at a good time. Hernando Cortes was also at court, reporting on the marvellous riches of the lands he had just conquered in Mexico. Hoping that he would do the same in Peru, the Emperor

Opposite: *Pizarro's route to Peru*

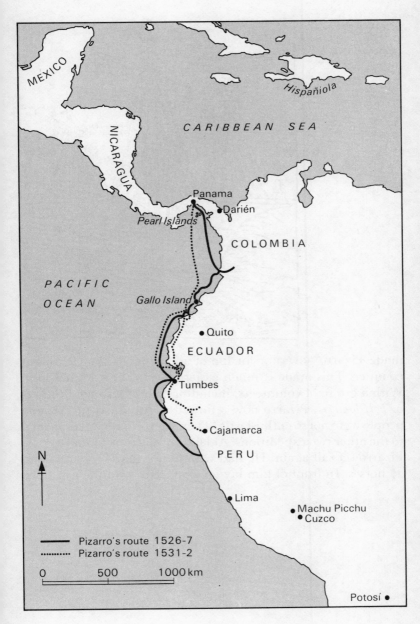

MEXICO

NICARAGUA

CARIBBEAN SEA

Hispañiola

Panama • • Darién
Pearl Islands

COLOMBIA

PACIFIC OCEAN

Gallo Island

• Quito

ECUADOR

Tumbes

• Cajamarca

N

PERU

• Lima

• Machu Picchu
• Cuzco

Pizarro's route 1526-7
.... Pizarro's route 1531-2

0   500   1000 km

Potosí •

57

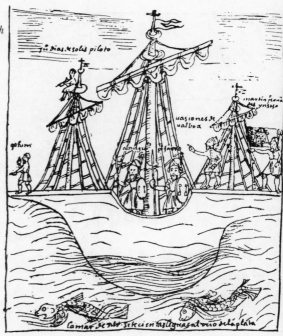

made Pizarro governor for life of all the lands that he might conquer. This made it much easier to get others to join him. With a group of volunteers, including four of his own brothers or *half-brothers*, Pizarro now returned to America. In Panama people were not so enthusiastic. They knew what had happened to the other two expeditions. At last, however, in January 1531, Pizarro set sail again. He had with him 3 ships, 180 men and 27 horses. In front of him lay an Empire of 10 million people.

8 Cajamarca

Pizarro could not have arrived in Peru at a better time. On his first visit to Tumbes four years earlier the Inca Emperor, Huayna Capac, lay dying in Quito. He was probably suffering from one of the diseases that the Spaniards had brought with them to the New World. Messengers came with news of the bearded strangers just before the Emperor died. These men, he told his nobles, must be the warriors of the god, Viracocha. When they came the Inca Empire would be at an end.

Huayna Capac had many sons and had not decided at the time of his death which of them was to follow him as Emperor. Without waiting to see if the other orejones agreed, one of these sons, named Huascar, made himself Emperor in Cuzco. Anyone who looked as if they were going to disagree was put to death. Only his half-brother, Atahualpa, who was the Governor of Quito, refused to obey him. War soon broke out between the two brothers. Many Indians, like Amaro, whom you read about in Chapter 6, were taken from their villages to join one or other of the armies. Atahualpa now claimed that he was the true Emperor and sent his troops against Cuzco. The fighting was still going on when Pizarro returned in 1531. Hearing of the arrival of the Spaniards, Huascar sent messengers to Pizarro, hoping the strangers would help him against Atahualpa. It was too late. Shortly afterwards Atahualpa's generals, moving southwards, met Huascar's army north of the capital, defeated it and took Huascar prisoner. His life was spared for the moment. Most of his wives and children, however, were brutally killed in front of his own eyes. The war of the two brothers was over, but Atahualpa had not yet been crowned. Many Indians hated him and were willing to help anyone, even the Spaniards, against him. Pizarro was indeed lucky to have arrived at this time.

Atahualpa was at Cajamarca, a town high up in the Andes, when he heard about the arrival of the Spaniards. He had gone there because of its hot springs, to bathe a wound he had received during the recent wars. What was he to do about these bearded strangers? He had not forgotten his father's warning, but he was curious. He had a huge army and a vast Empire. He was the Son of the Sun. What could a tiny force of strangers do to hurt him? When he heard that Pizarro was on his way to Cajamarca, he decided therefore not to stop him. He sent messengers with gifts, telling Pizarro that he wished to be his friend.

Pizarro also had a difficult decision to make. He had landed on the coast of Ecuador, just north of the Equator. He had stayed there for a few months, and then marched southwards under a burning sun to Tumbes. It was here that he learnt that Atahualpa was only 340 kilometres away. Pizarro expected some more Spaniards to join him soon. Should he march and meet Atahualpa while he was still quite close, or should he wait until he had a bigger army? He decided to risk it. On 24 September, 1532, the march to Cajamarca began. Pizarro was leading an army of 110 footsoldiers, 67 horsemen and 3 gunners. It was a tiny force to set against the might of the whole Inca Empire.

The footsoldiers wore helmets, as in the picture on page 71. They mostly carried swords and pikes. About twenty of them had crossbows or *arquebuses*, a kind of old gun, instead. Most of the Spaniards were not soldiers by trade. They were ordinary men: merchants, tailors, shoemakers, clerks, sailors. They were ready to fight if this were necessary to make their fortune. They had also brought many Negro and Indian slaves with them from Panama. The Negroes came originally from West Africa and had been brought to the New World by slave traders. The Indians were from tribes that the Spaniards had conquered further north. Both Indians and Negroes worked as servants, carrying the food and equipment, helping the Spaniards in battle, though not fighting themselves.

Travelling on the Inca roads Pizarro and his men marched deeper and deeper into Atahualpa's Empire. It was not an easy journey, even with the roads to help them. In places the ground was so steep and the path so narrow that they had to walk in single file. At night it was bitterly cold. All the time they were on the lookout for an ambush. One Indian chief whom they tortured told them how Atahualpa had boasted to kill every one of them. There was no ambush, however, and no sign of Atahualpa's army. More messengers arrived, but only to bring gifts and to invite the Spaniards to visit the Emperor in Cajamarca. Pizarro was worried but did not think of turning back. The prize was too great.

On the morning of 15 November, from the mountain slopes above the town, Pizarro and his men looked down on Cajamarca, 2,740 metres above sea-level. Beyond the town, on the grassy plain, were the tents of the Inca army. They had been warned that the town was empty, that all the people had gone to the Emperor's camp. It must have been a strange feeling as they marched through the narrow dusty streets, looking, listening, wondering if this were some kind of a trap. Pizarro chose for their barracks a large square, surrounded by walls and houses, and with only two entrances. His plan was now to persuade Atahualpa to visit him there and take him prisoner. He sent one of his captains, Hernando de Soto, to Atahualpa's camp to ask the Emperor to come into the town and talk with him. Atahualpa promised to visit Pizarro on the next day. He was obviously very interested in their horses and asked one of the Spaniards to gallop his horse in front of him. Atahualpa himself showed no fear at this strange sight, but thirty or forty Indians ran away in terror. According to one Spaniard who was in Cajamarca at the time, Atahualpa put all these men to death as soon as de Soto and his companions had left the camp. He was not going to allow anyone to show the Spaniards that they were afraid.

The Spaniards got up early the next morning, made their

plans and then knelt down in the square to hear the Latin *Mass*. They were, of course, Catholic Christians like most people in Europe at this time. Father Valverde, the priest who said Mass that morning in Cajamarca, was always reminding them that the Indians were wicked *heathens* who worshipped the Sun. This perhaps made them feel better about the dreadful things they were going to do. After Mass Pizarro hid all his men and the two cannons inside the buildings around the square. Then they waited for Atahualpa. They waited and they waited, as the sun moved slowly across the sky above the little town. It was not until late afternoon that the lookout saw the huge Indian army marching across the plain towards them. It was a terrifying sight. First came the road-sweepers, brushing the path along which the Emperor was to travel. Behind them were three *squadrons* of soldiers, most or perhaps all of them unarmed. Above them all was the Emperor carried high in his litter, and surrounded by his most important chieftains. They all marched slowly into the empty square and stopped. Atahualpa stayed inside his litter. Only Father Valverde came forward to meet him, making a long speech in which he asked Atahualpa to become a Christian and to accept the Spanish King as his lord. He spoke of course in Spanish. When he had finished the young Indian interpreter that Pizarro had brought with him from the coast translated the speech into Quechua. The interpreter however knew very little Spanish and very little Quechua. Atahualpa cannot have understood very much of what he was saying. He did ask Father Valverde how he knew all these things about God and Jesus Christ. Father Valverde gave him the prayer book that he was holding. Atahualpa looked carefully at each page and then flung it down to the ground, saying that 'it said nothing to him'. At this Valverde rushed back towards Pizarro, shouting 'At them! At them!' Pizarro made a signal and from inside the houses around the square the cannons boomed, the arquebuses crackled and the horsemen charged out from their hiding places into the crowds of defenceless Indians. The Indians were taken completely by surprise.

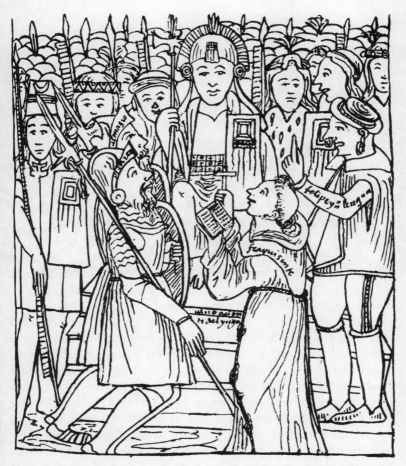

Pizarro and Almagro kneel at Atahualpa's feet. Father Valverde asks him to become a Christian. How does this version of the meeting at Cajamarca (by Guamán Poma) differ from the version in the text?

They fought fiercely to protect their Emperor, but could not stop the Spaniards from dragging Atahualpa by his hair out of the litter. Hundreds, perhaps thousands, of them were hacked to pieces by the Spanish swords. Many fled in panic, even breaking down the walls in their desperate rush to get

A later German drawing of the events at Cajamarca. How does this drawing tell a different story from the one you have read in this chapter?

away. As they ran across the plain the Spanish horsemen gave chase, killing many more. Not a single Spaniard was killed.

Pizarro could hardly believe his success. He had taken Atahualpa prisoner and destroyed the Inca army. If he was careful, the whole Empire might soon be his. On the following day his men marched out to the abandoned Inca camp and looted all the gold and silver they could find. Seeing their love for precious metals, Atahualpa now offered the Spaniards a *ransom* – a large room filled with gold and silver. When it was full, to the height of his hands above his head, the Spaniards were to release him. Pizarro of course agreed, for the sake of the gold. During the next few weeks, while Atahualpa learnt to play chess and cards, Indians from all over the Empire made their way along the Inca roads, bringing gold and silver to Cajamarca. Three Spaniards went to Cuzco to help speed up its collection. They were the first to visit the holy city. On their way they met Huascar, still a prisoner. Huascar offered

*An Inca statue made out of gold.
Statues like this were probably
part of the ransom that
Atahualpa paid Pizarro*

them even more gold than his half-brother had done. When
Atahualpa heard of this, fearing the Spaniards would make a
deal with him instead, he sent orders for him to be executed at
once.

Eventually the room was almost full. The ransom had been
paid. The Spaniards melted down all the gold and silver and
divided it among themselves. Atahualpa of course was not
released. The Spaniards could not decide what to do with him.
Some of them, like de Soto, had got to know and like him.
Others just wanted him out of the way now that the gold had
all come in. Pizarro decided to kill him. He sent de Soto off
on an expedition. As soon as he had gone, he accused Atahualpa
of organising a revolt against the Spaniards, tried him, and
sentenced him to death by burning. For an Inca there could
not have been a worse way to die. If the body were burnt,
they believed, the soul would not be able to live in the next

The death of Atahualpa. How can you tell that the German artist who drew this had never been to Peru?

world. In return for a different kind of death, Atahualpa agreed to become a Christian. Father Valverde baptised him. He was then tied to a post and strangled. He died with great courage.

With Atahualpa's death the Inca Empire came to an end. The people were used to obeying orders. Now that no orders came they were lost and did not know what to do. This is why it was possible for so few Spaniards to take over such a vast Empire so quickly. Pizarro now marched southwards to Cuzco. His brother, Hernando, had meanwhile gone down to the coast and persuaded the chieftains to accept Spanish rule. Further north other captains took over Quito, Huayna Capac's old capital. The Inca Empire had almost collapsed. A new Spanish Empire was being made.

9 *Peru after the Conquest*

The fighting however was not over when Pizarro marched into the Inca capital in 1533. In fact it was only just beginning. For the next few years large parts of Peru were destroyed by wars between Spaniards and Indians and wars among the Spaniards themselves. Many Indians died in battle and from disease, starvation and ill-treatment. In 1530 there had been

Guamán Poma shows how some Spaniards ill-treated the Indians after the conquest

perhaps ten million Indians in Peru. By 1560 there cannot have been more than two and a half million. These were the results of the Spanish conquest. Even some Spaniards were appalled at what they had done. As one of them said at the time, 'the Spaniards did more damage in four years alone than the Inca rulers did in four hundred'.

The death of Atahualpa was a great shock to many Indians. As the Son of the Sun he had protected them from the gods. They had to work hard, but their rulers looked after them in return. Now this had ended. The whole world seemed to be collapsing around them. They soon learnt what hard masters the Spaniards were. Pizarro and his followers took away their land, forbade them to worship their gods and often treated them very brutally. They now paid taxes to the Spanish King and the Spanish settlers, to the priests and the new Spanish officials, as well as to their old chieftains. Some hoped that their old gods were just sleeping and would one day rise up again and punish the Spaniards and their gods. Others turned to drunkenness and to chewing *coca* leaves, to escape from their miserable lives. Many seem to have killed themselves. Some, however, fought against the Spaniards. In 1536–7 an Indian army led by Manco Inca, one of the sons of Huayna Capac, laid siege to Cuzco. Manco had at first helped the Spaniards, thinking that they were the sons of Viracocha. They had treated him so badly that he had soon changed his mind. 'They are not the sons of Viracocha', he said, 'but of the Devil'. He and his men killed all the Spaniards they could find and then laid siege to Cuzco. Inside there were about three hundred Spaniards. For a whole year the Indians surrounded the city, firing burning torches on to the thatched roofs of the houses. Almost all the Spaniards were wounded at one time or another. Most of them slept in their armour with their horses saddled beside them, ready for the next Indian attack. Manco, however, was never strong enough to take the city. After a year help came to the besieged Spaniards and Manco returned once more into the mountains. The Indians were never quite so successful again. For nearly forty years Manco and his sons managed to hold out in the mountains north of Cuzco, living in places like the fortress at Machu Picchu and carrying out raids from time to time against the

The ruins of the Inca fortress of Machu Picchu

Spaniards. Not until 1572 was the last ruler of this little Inca kingdom, Tupac Amaru, captured by the Spaniards. He was taken to Cuzco to be publicly beheaded. The huge crowd of Indians gasped with horror as the executioner raised the sword above his head. The shock was almost as great as when Atahualpa had been killed forty years before. After 1572 there were no more Inca Emperors to trouble the new rulers of Peru.

As well as fighting the Indians the Spaniards also fought each other. The main quarrel was between Pizarro and his old friend, Diego de Almagro. It had started before the expedition even set out. Almagro was annoyed that Pizarro, 69 rather then himself, was going to be the governor of all the new lands. The quarrel was made worse at Cajamarca when Almagro and his men arrived too late to have much of a share in Atahualpa's ransom. In order to avoid a war Almagro agreed to go off and conquer Chile. He hoped to find there riches as great as those in Peru. He was away for nearly two years. During this time he marched thousands of kilometres over high mountains and across deserts. Many of the Indians he took with him died of cold and exhaustion. He found very little gold or silver and returned to Peru a disappointed man. The Indians were in revolt at this time. It was Almagro who drove Manco Inca away from Cuzco. He then decided to rule the city himself. He claimed that it was inside the area that the Spanish King had given to him. Pizarro, of course, objected and sent an army against Cuzco. Watched by thousands of Indians, the two sides met in battle outside the city. Almagro was the loser. Hernando Pizarro, Francisco's brother, took him prisoner and sentenced him to death. Almagro pleaded for his life on his knees, but Hernando was stern and told him to prepare for his death. Almagro was then strangled in prison. His followers never forgot how the Pizarros had treated their leader. Three years later they had their revenge, bursting into Francisco Pizarro's house in Lima and stabbing the old man to death. Although taken by surprise and outnumbered, he still managed before he died to kill at least two of his attackers. It was a violent death, after a life full of violence.

Wars among the Spaniards continued on and off for a few more years. The Indians, as you can imagine, suffered much more from the looting and killing than the Spaniards themselves. Finally, officials sent out from Spain managed to stop the fighting. They took away the lands of the worst offenders and made new laws that everyone had to obey. After 1548 Peru settled down at last to a period of peace.

Indian revolts and *civil wars* did not stop the Spaniards from setting out in search of new lands. Some went northwards into Colombia. Others went to the south, to Chile again or over the Andes into Argentina. You can see where these

fran her nâdes.

fortaleza de
los antepaza
dos yngas
puccra.

estemato cien
hombres

*Spaniards fighting each other. Compare this with the picture of Indians fighting on
page 19*

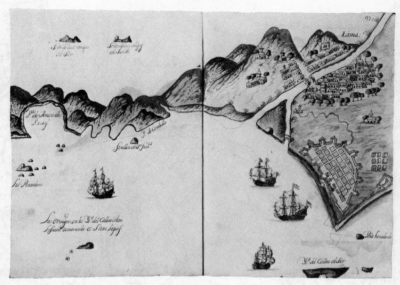

A Spaniard drew this plan of Lima not long after the city was founded

countries are on the map on page 4. There were many stories of gold and silver and rich kingdoms hidden in the jungle. Some of these rumours led the Spaniards over the Andes into the wet hot jungles of the Amazon basin that the Incas had never managed to conquer. Here many of them lost their way or returned only after terrible sufferings. It was during one of these expeditions that a group of Spaniards, unable to go back the way they had come, came across the great Amazon river. They sailed eastwards for months and months until at last, nearly 5,000 kilometres from Peru, they reached the Atlantic Ocean.

Inside Peru itself the Spaniards were building towns like Lima and setting up town councils to run them. In Potosí, in what is now Bolivia, they opened what soon became the largest silver mine in the world. They built churches and *monasteries* and sent priests and monks round the country to baptise the Indians. More and more Spaniards made the long journey out to Peru. Some of them, like Pizarro's followers, became big landowners with large numbers of Indians to work for them. Others set up in business as merchants, lawyers, craftsmen, doctors and shopkeepers. Many brought their Negro slaves with them. Once the country was settled Spanish women came out as well. There were still, however, far fewer women then men. Many of the Spanish men therefore had Indian wives. Their children, part Indian and part European, became know as *mestizos*.

The Indians – those that were left – did not find it easy to live in the new country that the Spaniards were making. Some became Christians or at least agreed to be baptised. Some learnt Spanish. A few, especially perhaps the old chieftains, began to copy the Spanish style of dress, riding round on horseback in Spanish hats and boots. But many of them lived in the old way as best they could. So there were two worlds in Peru after the conquest: the world of the Spaniards and the world of the Indians. The mestizos did not fit easily into either. There were always far more Indians than Spaniards, but the Spaniards were very much in charge. Even after Peru and Bolivia broke away from Spain and became countries on their own, the descendants of the old Spanish conquerors still ruled. The Indians, however, never forgot that they were once the masters of this land. Even today, in towns and villages in some parts of Peru and Bolivia, the people dress up every year as Incas and Spaniards and act out the story of the conquest. Sometimes in Bolivia the Spaniards have modern army uniforms and the Inca princesses wear sunglasses and carry umbrellas. The story, however, remains the same. When Atahualpa is put to death the princesses cry out in horror, just as they did in Cajamarca all those years ago.

How Do We Know?

We know less about the Incas than we do about many other peoples, such as the Romans, partly because the Incas never learnt to write. No one wrote down the story of Topa Inca's marches. We have to rely on the memories of old people who told the Spaniards what had happened. They had probably forgotten many things, or the Spaniards might have misunderstood what they were saying. There is a lot, however, that we do know, especially about their everyday life. Many Inca buildings and objects have survived. By studying their pottery and clothes, their quipus, their roads, terraces, fortresses and temples we can learn about how the Incas lived. Archaeologists are finding out more and more about the size of their cities, how their irrigation worked, their methods of building, the kind of crops they grew.

There are also many accounts of Indian life written after the conquest. Spanish officials toured the country finding out as much as they could. Spanish soldiers and priests also wrote down what they saw. The *Chronicle of Peru* by the soldier, Pedro Cieza de León, is an interesting account. Some Indians, like Guamán Poma de Ayala, learnt to read and write. He sent his *New Chronicle* to the King of Spain in 1615. You have already seen some of his pen and ink drawings in this book. These tell us a great deal about everyday life. There is an English translation of part of Guamán Poma, called *Letter to a King* (George Allen and Unwin, 1978). Garcilaso de la Vega, whom you have also heard about, was the son of an Inca princess and a Spanish conqueror. He wrote his *Royal Commentaries* while living in Spain as an old man. We have to be very careful about using accounts like these. Spaniards who knew very little Quechua often misunderstood what they were told. Some Indians wrote to please their new masters. Others, like Garcilaso, tried very hard to show what marvellous rulers the Incas had been. Some of what they say therefore is rather one-sided.

We can also learn something by watching the plays and dances about the conquest that the Indians still perform. Some of these seem to have been made up at the time. The Indians have handed them down by word of mouth from one generation to another. They help to tell us how they felt all those years ago when the Spaniards first appeared and their whole world collapsed.

There are quite a few accounts of the conquest by Spaniards who took part themselves, or who arrived in Peru shortly afterwards. These again are not always very accurate. Writers often exaggerated the number of their enemies or in trying to tell a good story forgot altogether what actually happened. The best, the *History of the Discovery and Conquest of Peru* (Penguin, 1968) is by a Spanish official, Agustín de Zárate. We also have some of the letters that Spaniards wrote at the time. These were not written to be published and often give a very different story. You can find some of these in *Letters and People of the Spanish Indies*, by Enrique Otte (Cambridge University Press, 1976).

For life in Peru after the conquest there are all kinds of documents that historians can look at: work contracts, tax lists, church records. Many of these have not yet been used. There is still a lot we do not know about the history of Peru.

Two useful modern books are *Everyday Life of the Incas*, by A. Kendall (Batsford, 1973) and *The Conquest of the Incas*, by J. Hemming (Macmillan, 1970). *Latin America from Conquest to Independence* by J. R. Fisher (Hart-Davis Educational, 1971) continues the story after the conquest.

Things To Do

1. Make a frieze to illustrate some of the things that Topa Inca did on his campaigns.
2. Act out a scene in the Emperor's palace in Cuzco with different people being orejones, messengers etc.
3. Make your own quipu and use it to send a message to someone.
4. Make a model of the group of huts in which Amaro and Qori lived.
5. Imagine you are a Spaniard with Pizarro's expedition in 1531–2. Write a diary of your journey from Panama to Cajamarca.
6. Imagine you are a Spaniard writing home about what happened at Cajamarca on 15 and 16 November 1532. Then imagine you are an Inca noble who managed to escape. Write about the same events from the Inca point of view.
7. You are one of the three Spaniards who visited Cuzco shortly after Pizarro's arrival in Cajamarca. Write a report to Pizarro, describing what you have seen.
8. Find out more about the fortress at Machu Picchu, who lived there and when and how it was discovered.
9. Imagine you are one of the Indian family you read about in Chapter 6. Describe what happened to you after 1531.
10. Find out more about the Spaniards who explored the River Amazon. You can read some of their own accounts in *Journeys down the Amazon* by J. M. Cohen (Charles Knight, 1975).
11. Find out as much as you can about modern Peru, the towns, the countryside, farming, fishing, industry, transport. How does what happened in 1532 still affect people today?

Glossary

adobes, clay bricks dried in the sun

alpaca, South American animal, similar to a llama, used for its wool

ancestor, someone who long ago belonged to the same family or people as oneself

archaeologists, men or women who find out about life long ago by digging up and studying the things that people left behind them

arquebus, old gun, fired from the shoulder

balsa, kind of wood that floats well

bitumen, black substance, like tar

bolas, strings with balls or stones attached, used as a weapon by the Indians

bronze, brown-coloured metal made by mixing tin and copper

chicha, drink made from maize

chili pepper, small, red, very hot vegetable, used in cooking for flavouring

civil war, war between two groups of the same people

coca, plant whose leaves are used to make the drug cocaine

colony, group of people who have left their homes to live in lands that they or their rulers have conquered

convent, place where women (called 'nuns') can spend their lives away from the world praying to God

Coya, most important wife of the Inca Emperor

descendant, someone belonging to the same family or people as someone else who lived a long time ago

to domesticate, to tame an animal so that it is no longer wild

embarked, went on board ship

fertiliser, something added to the land to make crops grow better

fortified, strengthened against attack

guano, bird droppings from islands off the coast of Peru, used as manure

halberd, long weapon, part axe and part spear

half-brothers, brothers who have the same father and different mothers, or the same mother and different fathers

heathens, people who are not Christians

hoe, tool used for breaking up the soil and for weeding

House of the Sun, temple of the Sun God in Cuzco

to irrigate, to get water to the land by means of ditches

innumerable, so many that they cannot be counted

to joust, to fight on horseback with blunted weapons, as a sport

litter, kind of vehicle carried on men's shoulders

llama, South American animal, a member of the camel family

maize, food plant, also called sweet corn or corn on the cob

mangrove, kind of tree that grows in dense clumps near water

Mass, Catholic church service

mestizo, person of mixed Spanish and Indian blood

mita, special work that all Indian men had to do for their Emperor

monastery, place where men (called 'monks') can spend their lives
  away from the world, praying to God

mortar, mixture (usually cement, sand and water) that holds stones
  together in a building

mummies, preserved bodies of dead people

orejones, pronounced 'orrayhonays' – the most important Inca nobles

plateau, large, flat piece of land, often high up

puma, American lion

puna, high plateau in the Andes mountains

pyramid, large building that comes to a point and has four triangular
  sides

Quechua, pronounced 'ketch-oo-a' – the language spoken by the
  Incas and by most Peruvian Indians today

quinua, pronounced 'kee-noo-a' – a kind of rice grown in Peru

quipu, pronounced 'kee-poo' – strings used by the Incas for counting

ransom, payment to people who have captured someone. In return,
  they are supposed to let this person go

to sacrifice, to offer a thing or a person to a god; a sacrifice is the thing
  or person offered

sluice-gate, gate across a ditch or stream that can be opened or shut
  to control the flow of water

sorcerer, someone who practises magic

squadron, part of an army

taklla, foot plough

triumph, victory procession by an army that has just won a war

vicuña, South American animal, similar to the llama. It lives wild
  on the high plateau

Viracocha, important Inca god, who was expected (one day) to
  return to Peru. The Incas thought of him as a man with a beard

Index

Acknowledgements

We are grateful to the following for permission to reproduce photographs:

Archivo General de Indias, Seville, page 53; Stephen Benson, pages 16 and 25; Biblioteca Nacional, Madrid, page 72; Bodleian Library, Oxford, pages 54 and 64; British Museum, page 22; Camera Press, pages 11 left (photo Patrick Knight) and 37 (photo Suzanne Hill); FAO, page 47 (photo Peyton Johnson); Robert Harding Picture Library, page 69; Maritiem Museum Prins Hendrik, Rotterdam, page 55; Mary Evans Picture Library, page 66; Marion Morrison, pages 7 and 9; Tony Morrison, pages 10, 12, 13 and 30; J. H. Steward, *Handbook of South American Indians, Volume II*, U.S. Government Publications Office, Washington, 1946, page 14 below; Rev. George T. Thomson, page 11 right; Werner Forman Archive, pages 14 above (Dallas Museum of Fine Arts) and 65 (Museum of American Indian, New York).

The line illustrations on pages 19, 21, 27, 29, 33, 34, 39, 41, 42, 45, 48, 49, 58, 63, 67, 71 and cover are from Felipe Huamán Poma de Ayala's *Nueva Corónica y Buen Gobierno*, the original of which is in Det Kongelige Bibliotek, Copenhagen. They are taken from the new, redrawn edition published by the Institut d'Ethnologie, Paris, 1936 and 1968.

The diagrams on pages 8 and 36 are simplified versions of artwork from A. Kendall, *Everyday Life of the Incas*, Batsford.